From the Altar of the Land

Other Collections by D. Walsh Gilbert

Finches in Kilmainham

Misneach: A Story of Kidnap, Enslavement, and Colonialism

Deirdre

Ransom

imagine the small bones

[M]AR[Y]

Once the Earth had Two Moons

Bleat & Prattle

no mother but the sky

From the Altar of the Land

poems

D. Walsh Gilbert

GRAYSON BOOKS
West Hartford, Connecticut
graysonbooks.com

From the Altar of the Land
Copyright © 2025 by D. Walsh Gilbert
Published by Grayson Books
West Hartford, Connecticut
ISBN: 979-8-9985883-1-0
Library of Congress Control Number: 2025913107

Book and Cover Design by Cindy Stewart
Cover Image: Jacquelinegillamfairchild via pixabay.com

Characters, place names, and incidents in this collection of poems are the work of the author's imagination. Any resemblance to persons living or dead is coincidental. However, the events portrayed are based on actual events reported by historical witnesses and recorded in many sources.

"I hope that real love and truth
are stronger in the world
than any evil or misfortune …"
                —Charles Dickins, *David Copperfield*

"Poetry begins where the language starts,
in the shadows and accidents
of one person's life."
                —Eavan Boland

Dedicated
to all the single mothers and babies of Ireland lost to each other

Contents

Vocabulary and Punctuation   10
Foreword   11
The Meaning of Sean Nós   13

1959
Love's Fairytale   17
Ten Commandments to the Women of Holy Catholic Ireland, 1959   18
Dreaming that the Green Can Blossom   19
As if Young Love Could Heal   20
What to do?   21
Love Letter Folded into Eighths   22
He's as fifteen as the likes of you!   23
The Ache   24
Into the Mother and Baby Home   25
James, Broken   26
From Ponytail to Chopped   27
New Friends   28
Aisling Tells All: One Ordinary Girl on One Extraordinary Day   29
Mae's Child is Taken Away   31
Why Become Invisible   32
The Earth Overturns   33
Bothering the Stones   35
Michael James Quinn   36
All the Voices Silenced   37
Aisling Speaks   38
Come with us, dear Michael   39

2024
In the Pubs, Nightly   43
Called Home   44
Between Here and There   45
Imperfect Lambs   46
Eleanór a Rún   47

As If the Dirt Was Just Sugar   48
James Teaches Cara to Make Irish Stew   50
Postcard Home   51
Putting Pieces Together   52
James and Michael James Trace the Past   53

Notes   55
Sources for Research   60
Acknowledgments   61
About the Author   63

Vocabulary and Punctuation

Aisling	Girl's name	ASH-lin
Amhrán Mhuighinse	Title of a song	OR-unn WIN-sha
Anach Cuain	Title of a song	AN-ock COO-in
Bodhrán	A drum	BŌ-run
Céilí	A dance	KAY-lee
Clochar	A nunnery or convent	CLŌ-ker
Craic	Fun	KRAK
Didean	A surname	DEE-dun
Eleanór a Rún	Title of a song	EL-i-nor ah ROON
Gardaí	Guards or police	GAR-day
Glenveagh	A park in County Donegal	Glen-VAY
Mícheál Séamus	Boy's names	MEE-haul SHAY-muss
Mullaghmore	A village in County Sligo	Mull-lay-more
Poitín	Liquor made from potatoes	PAW-cheen
Sean nós	A kind of vocal song	SHA-nōs
Sleán	A spade to cut peat	Shlawn
Slieve Liag	A mountain in County Donegal	Shleev Leeg
Uilleann	A musical instrument	ILL-ee-an

Foreword

The latest collection of poems from D. Walsh Gilbert comprises a verse-story of extraordinary power and beauty about the fate of single mothers and their babies in Ireland in 1959. The story of Aisling and James is heart-rending and reflects the reality visited upon a significant number of others in that relatively recent era.

The beauty of the imagery stands in stark contrast to the cruelty experienced by the young couple. The poems are literally rooted in the landscape: the "quaggy bog," the well, the potato field, and references to the authentic vegetation of these places: the plump blackberries, their thorns, the "fairy thimbles." Authenticity is further enhanced by the author's use of Gaelic (Irish) words and by references to Irish traditional music. This imagery is contrasted with refences to a "Morris Minor," "Sweet Afton" (cigarettes), and the music of Elvis, so that the reader is made aware that these events are set in modern times.

The cruelty experienced by Aisling and her fellow-inmates in the "Bally House" is described by references to shorn hair, physical and emotional coldness, bad food, and the unbearable grief of losing their babies. The redemptive section which closes the collection is credible and unsentimental.

As well as being a collection of moving and memorable poems, this is also a work of considerable scholarship. The author has consulted an impressive collection of sources and provides comprehensive footnotes to them.

This unique and original collection is outstanding in its emotional power, use of imagery, and meticulous research. It demands to be read, and will leave the reader shaken, moved, and ultimately uplifted.

—Rose Malone, Sancho Panza Literary Society
Dublin, June 2025

The Meaning of Sean Nós

It's the love of family. Always
the family.

And utterly inseparable, the song
of the family—voices
planted in fruitful patchwork.

Stitched by legend, myth,
and ritual into shades
of green and shadow.

It's the only solid footing
found in a land's quaggy bog

where a woman could disappear.

Here, eyes wide open, she tiptoes
across the softness, and listens

for the knell of the expunged—
a ballad, a lullaby, a dirge.

1959
Rawnshinshare
County Leitrim, Ireland

Love's Fairytale

Once upon a time, James Coppinger
knew when he was home—

the warmth of welcome arms,
the absence of loneliness,

the security of a skirt's tweed
of woven flax and felted wool.

Home was the fur of the newborn
rabbit in the dew-damp fields,

and the taste of rain beading the inner
wrist of his beloved, Aisling.

He found his sustenance
in the heart-shaped birthmark behind her left ear

and on the curve
of her hip, a hillock he could palm,

and hold and hold …
and call his home, while knee-deep

in the spikes of fledgling barley
growing in the shade of the steeple.

Ten Commandments to the Women of Holy Catholic Ireland, 1959

1. Harmony, morality, and the social order of Ireland are rewarded to those born responsibly legitimate and baptized into the Roman Catholic Church. The State will not challenge this mandate of the church and defers to her reason, virtue, and integrity.
2. Shame, disgrace, slander, and stain will come to the woman who lies with a man before the sacrament of holy wedlock.
3. Dishonor and humiliation will fall on the family of the single mother—on her father and on her mother for their failings of a good home.
4. The sinner despised, the indecent, the disrespectable, the prostitutes who are burdens to our world must separate from the righteous.
5. The woman fallen into inferior status shall have no rights to care, shelter, or familial ties and will be isolated. The presence and the sight of sin will be hidden from all those more holy. The fathers will be exonerated.
6. Only confession, control, punishment, and sufficient suffering of the female offender, no matter her age, will reform and save her soul from the fires of Hell.
7. Repeat-offenders will be condemned as mentally incompetent and may be committed and removed without notice.
8. The birth of mixed races will be segregated from others—subject to strict division from the civil and the pure.
9. No child, born to a Catholic, shall become Protestant.
10. No mother made filthy may keep her spawn of Satan.

Dreaming that the Green Can Blossom

Aisling Quinn halves the seed potato, its sprout
drawn from the round body itself, without
sunlight, best kept in a cool dark barrel.

When she thinks of James, she giggles.
She remembers two picnics and a set dance—
a reel and swing with its céili hold,
the pub at the crossroads with its good
oak floor, his strong farmer arms.
They'd shared mince, mushy peas, custard.

She'd laughed with him when his bicycle tire
went flat—a slow leak—she was riding
on his handlebars, schoolbooks in his basket.
A dip or two in the river while fishing.

Soon she'll be ready to hill the potatoes, the living
part underground, shoots stretched toward light.
A spud taps vigor from inside its wrinkly self
and grows. You never know how much you get.

She can't wait for their lavender flowers.
Roots to come, mounds to build.
Aisling's kept the secret of their romance—
kisses behind the pig shed, promises to meet.
They circle together like bees before thunder.

James' touch to her hand plants an empty field.
To her, the priest at Sunday Mass has gone silent.
Today, she buries eager buds in loose rich dirt,
fingernails blackened—her blue eyes closed.

As if Young Love Could Heal

You cup the vivid ember
in your naked palm
and close your fingers over it.
The flesh will burn.
Breathe deep
once, thrice—try to let go.
Patch the scar with raindrops.
There will be sizzle.
Then seal it with the messy tears
from a milkweed's broken stem.
It will be sticky.
Blood surfaces again. Call it
a tattoo. Call it a cattle brand.
You may not be able to erase it.
Some reckon love as sin.
You offer songs of dismissal. Crawl
along lamentation's path
looking for a river, an exit,
a tributary to the sea
even if you must stagger.
You will stagger.
Be fully on your knees.

What to do?

Aisling sits on her hands, unbalanced
on a raggedy three-legged stool
tufted with horsehair and sacrifice.

Set on the iron Aga, her blackened kettle
is starting to boil. The whistle
at its pouring mouth fills with steam.

She knows bran flour struggles to rise
in its loaf pan, but will finally swell
into shape. Then a hollow tap to proof it.

The baked crust hardens when the bread
is turned directly to the oven rack—
the sweet scent of it finally freed.

Her bleeding stopped six months ago.
And now she waits … fifteen years old,
and the eldest in a family already ten.

Despite James' gentle touch and tender love,
her Mam disapproves—forbidden
fruit ever sweeter as any Eve would know.

Aisling tears a ragged corner from the perfect
loaf, squeezes it in her fist, and flings
the ruin in the sink. She cries.

The coals glow hot in the firebox,
a snapping red so alive—it would only take
a moment to tuck her apron strings inside,

to end this shame and mortal sin in Hell.

Love Letter Folded into Eighths

Dearest Aisling,

In love with this lane, this gentle day, and you, I beg you meet me
where the cobbles end and the waters of the well begin. Here, we begin.
When the blackberries are plump, the thorns are worth the risk.
Marry me under the setting sun near midnight while the Fairy Thimbles
bloom and the air shifts toward another meadow. It would be ours, our
field already ripe. We'll find our way through bramble, over hedgerow,
and beyond the smoke of incense burned by hags and priest. Our fire
kindles still. Marry me and come away new-sparkling. The nettle soup
repays the sting of its leaf. Darkness deserves its moon. My heart breaks
without you, my hearth, my bread. Wander with me. Tread through
the ghosts holding down your heels. Barefoot, we escape.

Evermore,
your James

He's as fifteen as the likes of you!

Mrs. Quinn hauls Aisling by the hair
toward Father Dunn, pot-bellied, bald,
ancient to the village. He is standing
on the stone steps of the church,
his hands and fingers entwined
with a rosary of Connemara marble—
dull beads clasped against his black
robe. He prays for their safety
'from the snares of the Devil,
who wanders the world seeking
the ruin of souls.' The smell
of incense, wet wool, and candle wax
seeps from him—one who sought
God living in 'the existence, order,
and beauty of the world He made.'

To the fearful and the poor, this situation
is no reflection of God's wisdom and design—
Mrs. Quinn's child is with child.
Red-faced, clandestine, and sickened
with disgust, Mrs. Quinn shoves Aisling
through the alcove. Through its door. Says,

> *We'll tell your Da that you've a job*
> *as a kitchen maid in an England town.*
> *Father O'Hara out of Bricknell*
> *posts a letter with the Queen's stamp*
> *in three months' time—*
> *'tis the plan—he'll say you ran away.*
> *Don't be coming back to us.*
> *Ye gone.*

The priest closes his eyes. A nod.
And he makes the sign of the cross.

The Ache

Where do those abandoned go

when the hole in the earth has no bottom?
How can good-bye last forever?

There is so much to learn
by the bruised mint left to grow

between the stacking stones. No one
can wash off its oil.

Absence carries its own perfume.

Once a child leaps within its mother's womb,
can she declare it a stillborn lamb?

When does the trembling stop?

There must be a name for a mother's ache
left when her family walks off in the dark.

The word must sound like smoke
leaving a dying fire—soot drifts with it.

It must echo the weakness of one figure
cut from its string of paper dolls.

Into the Mother and Baby Home

'Thou shall not'
        to the Garden of Love.

Father Dunn's knock on the oakwood door
of the Bally House of Milk and Bread
sounds hollow. Nothing's heard from within.
But its polished-bronze knob eventually turns.

Sister Agnes of the Blessed Angels of Clochar
reaches for Aisling's elbow to guide her
over the threshold.

> *Thank you, Father.*
> *No donation from the family?*
> *Can we offer you a tea brack*
> *freshly made today?*

He always accepts on a cool Belleek plate
as thin and creamy as the porcelain skin
of any child's face. Then, Aisling is gone—

taken by a fluttering black bird. Any crumbs
she'd left to find her way back are eaten
by this crow who strips her fully naked
and leaves a dress as large as a shroud nearby.

The bath water ripples in the enameled steel tub
as Aisling dips her shivering fingers in.

James, Broken

Broken as   his fiddle's bow
          without its strings of cat gut,

Gutted   as the hedgehog
          beneath a rabid fox's claw,

Clawed into tuneless   ribbons
          by secrecy and lies,

Lying helpless
          beneath the rowan tree—anonymous,

Anonymous as   the father
          of the moon and Milky Way,

Way   of any wayfarer
          without a waymark—only waylay

Laid before him
          every time   he looks for her.

From Ponytail to Chopped

Awakened at 6 AM, Aisling answers
to her new name, Rita. No one here keeps
the name she was given. Her ringlets sheared,
the nuns whisper in the halls,

> *No one can wipe the shame off you now.*
> *No one will want you.*
> *No one will want you.*

No one will want you
bounces off the plaster walls
as she finds her daily station—
boiling the linens of the newly delivered,
what no soap or lye could make clean.

Vivid red blood on sheets and knickers
has darkened into brown-black rust
as acrid as the iron bars of any prison cell.
This is the place for making penance—
where the gardaí dogs can track
the runaway by scent.

Cold bread and margarine for breakfast
before apocalyptic predictions about them all
are made at daily Mass—no rosaries enough
to hear the Virgin Mary answer back.

New Friends

Aisling could see one of her sisters in Mae's
blue eyes and square chin—a resemblance
comforting, and yet, a memory unsettling.

And her friend, Kathleen, wears the same dimples
as the youngest Quinn—not to be forgotten,
his pudgy knees once wrapped around her hip.

Her new companions fill in where love
was lost. At bedtime, Mae brushes what's left
of Aisling's hair, a hundred strokes,

smoothing wisps, spit-curling what she can,
while Kathleen giggles and veils her friend
with a white kitchen towel, pronouncing,

"for better, for worse, for richer, for poorer."

Then, Aisling upends a dried-willow broom—
a kindling bundle held to her chest. It stands in this day
for her future wedding's daisy bouquet.

"Have you come here freely and without reservation?"
"Will you accept children lovingly from God?"
And Aisling answers, "I will."

Aisling Tells All:
One Ordinary Girl on One Extraordinary Day

I wanted to show I wasn't afraid
so when Biddy waved me in from the open window
of the shiny ivory Morris Minor,
I squeezed beside her without thinking—already
muddied by agreement, already lost to the day.
Her neighbor was in the driver's seat.

Rich, Protestant, dangerous to befriend, Victoria
in her pencil skirt gripped her daddy's
steering wheel. Carroll's "Sweet Afton" unfiltered
was lit between her lips. That feg "the best
that money can buy." I could taste the smoke of it.

Me in cardigan and linen, Biddy wore her good
circle skirt—gathered full. No dangerous curves.
The flannel hit below her knees. Untapped joy
stretched from us like a starving man's reach.
Survival instincts lapsed at our parole. Hours stolen
from chores, from rules, from holy restraint.

We were away, and the hills baritoned along
with the radio cranked up to Elvis' croon—
to "Don't Be Cruel," to "All Shook Up,"
to "Love Me Tender," to "Jailhouse Rock."
The three of us knew all the words.

Then, a swig and a swallow at the Shaggy Pig Pub—
Irish dewy moonshine. Poitín loud
as any slide trombone. Where a boy called James
stringing his fiddle embraced me in his saddest song:
I thought I could live without romance … He said,
C'mere t'me. I want you. I need you. I love you.

I prayed for forgiveness alone to myself.
And the field sheep grew small in the distance.

Mae's Child is Taken Away

They've been together for twelve short weeks—
one plump baby girl in her mammy Mae's arms.
Where will you go, my wee Eileen?

With her eyes of blue and pink-rose cheeks,
a child to sweeten even byre or barn,
they've been together for twelve short weeks.

They've absorbed the deceit of the nuns' critiques,
those who'd promise a home and no more harm.
Where will you go, my wee Eileen?

Her infant to love and play-dabble in creeks
while watching wrens fly and honeybees swarm.
They've been together for twelve short weeks.

Now, she slips her in calico. Takes one last quick peek.
And hands her lamb to a pope-holy farmer.
Where will you go, my wee Eileen?

Mae—forced to do what the fierce nun speaks
with tears on booties knitted so warm.
They've been together for twelve short weeks.
Where have you gone, wee Eileen?

Why Become Invisible

The awful acid in the pit
of your stomach will begin
to gnaw, to make itself known.
There's a growl to it.
Says, *notice me.*
You are a witness.
You know things.
That's when invisible becomes
necessary. When a gradual
fading is protective—let
someone else be the center-
piece. Lean against
the wall, colored in dull paint.
Make no sound.
There are secrets around.
On the table, the cut apple
with its star-seeded core undraped
will draw the wasp.

The Earth Overturns

Under the stairs, Aisling gentles her friend, Kathleen,
whose son suffers fevers and withering marasmus.

Aisling sacrifices her last shred of brown bread, hidden,
crumbled in her apron pocket—something wanted, but shared—
something saved but given away.

Baby Liam dies in three days' time, too weak to suck
what wasn't there. Too soft. Too small. Too fragile.

And yet, Aisling's child moves again within her.

She never knew how much she could love one
little knob which could be an elbow or a knee pressed hard
against her growing belly. A little one who could be.

It feels like hunger. It feels like abundance.

More'n Kathleen deserved, says Sister Agnes to the digger
as she wraps the dead baby in a sheet ripped in half.
Bury him where he can't return.

And her man in green tweed digs a grave—somewhere
beyond the holly and the blushing rhododendron
out of bloom, out of sight. Without prayer or consecration.

He hums a lament of sean nós, *Anach Cuain*
a cappella with rhythmic shovelfuls of overturned earth.
He sings beyond the flowers where he can't be heard,

My pity tomorrow for the fathers and mothers,
Women and children who are weeping …

Soon, the locked door opens for the mother, Kathleen,
sent into her blue afternoon—opens
near surviving dandelion weeds and a finch's tangled nest

still gravid with its eggs. If she listens carefully,
if she ignores the hollow echo inside the home's long tunnel,
she can almost hear them crack.

Bothering the Stones

In the wild hallucinations of her final labor,
Aisling is delirious with searing, unmitigated pain,
taunted by a flapping blackbird asking,
Was your short pleasure worth this agony? Tell me now ...

This is surely the witch who made the village Hag Stone
from the hardened spit of cold coiled serpents
lying together—its hole pierced by the force of pointed tongues.
Snakes boring through flint and basalt.

Long ago, people walked three times around the stone egg
—the present, the past, and the future—
and when a couple clasped hands through the hole
in the stone, they were wed.
The old magic could never be broken.

Aisling and James had once passed fingers and fists
through the hole in a coastline hag stone,
but that pledge doesn't count anymore. Invalid.
Unsanctioned. Discredited love—blasphemous, ungodly.

Her newborn boy is small but robust. A tender
squalling abomination, she's told—*a wee bastard.*
And yet, held to her chest as tight as a wasp nest
caught in a whirlpool, Aisling vows she'll never let go.

Michael James Quinn

with first and final lines from "Glanmore Sonnets VI" by Seamus Heaney

He lived there in the unsayable lights.
He lived there piss-swaddled in a high-railed cot,
sucking his thumb and afraid of the sprites.
He lived there—his belly in a love-hungry knot.
He lived there rocking himself to sleep
waiting for Mammy to finish her chores,
a hallway to polish, pots to scrub, potatoes to heap
on a scullery shelf before sweeping the kitchen floor.
He lived there where no nun uttered his name,
nuzzled only by one who held him close
and knew someday—he'd be taken away.
He lived there, a rot on the scripture's rose,
as alone as fraught girls discarded to shrouds,
heard after dark above the drifted house.

All the Voices Silenced

No one knew how it started—a fire lit
among the rashers and the stone-cold eggs
in the scullery with its deep slop sinks
and soil pipes draining the filth and dirty
water hidden beneath the sunken floor.

Here was where the rabbits were bled.
Where the stink of turnips found the sewer.
Where potatoes boiled in a round copper pot
and a flat iron propped ready for linens.

Screams fill the room when the flames
grow hotter, when the napkins start to burn.
When Sister Agnes brusquely storms in.
When the door locks tightly behind her.

Four trapped girls snatch towels and aprons.
Soak them and hope to extinguish the fire.
This is a devil-fiend before them, this monarch of hell.
But the wild sparks spread, and the teens drop
to their knees to pray, *Sweet Jesus, save us.*

The blaze smells nothing like incense at Mass,
nothing like Christ's resurrection myrrh.
Then, Aisling starts to sing like the phoenix did
just before the bird on the pyre burned—singing alone
the old sean nós—*Amhrán Mhuighinse,* soft
with the drones of anguish behind her.
Soon, nothing to hear but the roof's collapse.

Aisling Speaks

an erasure of the poem "Immortality" by Katharine Tynan (1859-1931)

I have sunk,
                the grave and gloom
                    come.

            A weary head be laid
                without a stain.

The old mistakes are all undone—
                    sins
            wounds and scars.

Of me shall love be born anew.

            This poor body has died
and children's children yet to be
shall learn:

                the time
            shall be forgiven.

Come with us, dear Michael

To where the plains are flat
and the wind blows strong across them.
There lies the town of Old Millshawn
where a farmer can see for many miles
keeping watch over cattle and sheep.
There, the wheat never gets foul.
There, the apples are always ripe.
And the chapel prays Mary's rosary.
Come with us, dear Michael.

Where the ocean stretches, Cork to Boston,
a ship fitted with sails and rudders
to carry us to American shores.
Daylight and moonlight,
stars guiding our way,
you in your red flannel petticoat,
and Michael James Didean, your name.
No changeling.
No foundling.
Not anymore.
Patsy and Robert Didean will take you
where pink flowers line the cobblestones.
Come with us, dear Michael.

Cotter and stables will greet you
with horse and hen and fishing pole.
A boy with his raggedy hound
hunting pheasant and wood ducks
and sleeping the dreams of plenty.
Be barefoot in the summer,
woolen-wrapped at Christmas time.
Sing loud "Oh, Holy Night"
away in a manger new to you.
Come with us, dear Michael.

Good-bye to this Chapel of Precious Blood.
Good-bye to the Blessed Angels.
Good-bye to green fields,
to the wells and soft hills
swelling here in County Leitrim.
The tea is hot but sipped—
a donation made of £1000
for the sake of the poor mother's Home.

Burned sticks …
left on the family hearth …
It seems faeries have stolen the child
after all.
Come with us, dear Michael.
'For the world's more full of weeping
than you can understand.'

2024

In the Pubs, Nightly

James made his flute from a nightchurr's perch,
playing songs like bird-ghosts—the stillborn—alive in Limbo
crying for their mothers as he has begged for Aisling.

Sixty-five years, he's blown the notes of the Will-o'-the-Wisp,
the faeries' temptation to follow the lights toward
whatever it is that his wound remembers

—her curls of auburn, her wee pug nose, blue eyes,
her freckled neck and pink cheekbones—each tasted
with his kiss on those sweet days so long ago.

His grave is still earth-open. Waiting. His lips
never touched another as shimmering, scented of lily and milk.
They'd hadn't time to share their love, so he lingered, thinking

"all I want in this dark place is to have you here with me."

Called Home

Michael James believes his Irish name
sounds more genuine—Mícheál—
Mícheál Séamus Didean, adopted at birth
from the Blessed Angels of Clochar,
from somewhere—west coast, Ireland.

His mom and dad have been kind—
corned beef and cabbage, a university
education—but ancestry has haunted him.
As if a sod of turf, sleán-cut
and left to dry, he's stood motionless,
pleading for spark and vigor. Hungry grass
has spiraled in his marrow, left unmown.

The only cure is to visit—to feel
the swells from America find their way
Where the wandering water gushes
From the hills above Glen-Car.
He'll find the chapel there—small,
and utterly romantic, as the story goes,
when he flies to Tullen Strand in Tullaghan
and Ireland's Wild Atlantic Way.

Between Here and There

You expect to find
broken things,
given Ireland's strife.
But the land endures.
The owl, silent on the wing,
still calls out in the dark.
Still carries the field mouse
in its claws—
one thing broken,
one in flight.
Nocturne is like a requiem.
How heavy are empty arms?
No one wants to remember
how easy it is
to crush blackberries
while picking them.
You forget that hedge stones,
uncovered,
have been stacked
loosely into walls.
Climbed over,
some could roll away.
They don't go far.

Imperfect Lambs

Fresh wind whirls up the hillside as Heaney mentioned,
'Useless to think you'll park and capture it,' but Michael tries.

He hikes from the green and gold of Glenveagh's gardens
left behind by Black Jack Adair after bad famine times,

to the cliffs of Slieve Liag and the surf and headlands
where Mullaghmore meets the great, churning sea—

where the gray dolphins leap and the feral sheep roam,
each prancing its own wee dance. His daughter, Cara, has come

to hold the land's new lambs, puffed balls of wool wagging
their tails as they drink the cream of Connaught, Ireland.

Whistled to, a sheepdog separates the new-delivered lambs
for the shepherd to ink and tag and earmark as his own.

Some need to be bottle-fed, weaker than the rest. His callused
hands show Cara how to tip the nipple to their mouths,

how to cuddle them to her chest, and how they cuddle back.
But, the good dog, Jake, can't budge one mother protecting

her lamb born too small and three-legged, unable to stand.
Then, the winds of Ireland sting the old gorsed hill.

From their rookery of stony cribs, gulls circle for shallow fish.
The herder says, *Its mammy-ewe will never leave this one—*

He's all her own...'til someone comes and takes it away.

Eleanór a Rún

After all the honeyed meadows sleep—
when stars and dews collect,
when the magpie becomes dumb
and the larks have yet to speak,
then a golden time of Ireland glows.
A fiddler begins.
A bodhrán beats.
Tin whistles and pipes will sing.
And a solitary woman dressed in black
rises to tap, impromptu.
A session has begun.

In the Shaggy Pig Pub
with its snug upstairs,
with ale and stout,
and chips and cheese,
baked beans and toast to sop it up with,
there sits James Coppinger
as he has for forty years—
flute to his lips,
his flat cap in green box check
pulled low across his brow.

He closes his eyes
when the drone begins,
uilleann pipes on one long note,
and one lone voice in old sean nós
sings *Eleanór a Rún.*
Eleanor, My Secret Love—
her beauty enough
to bring bees off the loosestrife.
Eleanór a Rún
to bring the long-dead back to life.

As If the Dirt Was Just Sugar

Standing tall at the Shaggy Pig Pub, both regulars and guests
belt out *Ireland's Call* as if at a rugby match.

Some meet the barkeep and part with their pints
as if twirling the steps and clasping hands at a céilí dance.

Michael and Cara arrive late, but they soon join the craic.
Everyone knows the words "shoulder to shoulder" as well

as they know the tune to *When Irish Eyes Are Smiling.*
Everyone sings along. "There's whiskey in the jar."

James quiets when his flute needed tuning.
He's had a pint or two, and the faeries tickle his cheeks,

reddening them. The Tuatha need to be noticed and touched.

There, in the corner, at the mantle by the fire, a girl—about fifteen
he'd say. Something is familiar. Something he knows.

He watches her. The way she lifts her chin. The way
she tilts her head, smiles, gestures, walks—Aishling's way.

Aishling spooned from the grave as if the dirt was just sugar.

And James drops to his knees. His flute rolls away.
Cara, the ghost of Aishling, floats toward him—same hair, same eyes,

same wee pug nose, same heart-shaped birthmark on her neck.
From his pocket, he shows her Aishling's photo,

Cara's grandmother so similar in image and manner and laugh.
Coincidence or the concert of life's cycles? Could it be

James dares to ask. Could it truly be reincarnation?
What Michael and Cara soon come to believe.

James Teaches Cara to Make Irish Stew

The farming women in the country pull
the carrot, the onion, the purple turnip
from the altar of the land.
All of these grow underground. Unseen,
as are the women themselves,

as unseen as eggs held inside a pocket.
Fragile hen's eggs with no names.
One egg, identical to another.
The old ways did not include them.
The roots boiled soft in only salted water.

Add the seared lamb, cubed. It's tender.

In old Ireland, it was the man who held
the sun, the stars, a jacketed moon
in his palm. Only he could halve
the spud without getting cut.
The man was immune
to the slice of the church's knife.
        Do you see?
        Do you understand?

Now it's your turn
to spin the tip of a knife's steel blade,
to blind the potato's bitter eyes.
It leaves a black hole. A portal.
A thing to fall into. To stay forever.
We Irish finally learned
a stew thickens when tempered with egg.
Women make us hearty.
The soup has simmered for a bit.
Whisk a yolk or two. Stir them in well
to bind the broth.

Postcard Home

Dear Gramma,
James and Aisling?
And Clochar Blessed Angels?
Did you know
ANYTHING about this?
Love,
Cara

Mrs. Patsy Didean
4 Stag Fork Road
Millshawn, Ohio
USA

Putting Pieces Together

a cento

The young goldfinches
flutter down through the day for the first time
to find themselves among fallen petals.

What have they seen that they cannot forget—
all that space
the nighthawk plunges through,
homing.
All things counter, original, spare, strange.

There is something inside
each of us
that scurries toward the past.

We were lucky enough to sing the song once,
but we couldn't bring the dead any joy.

You'd already
snatched all the rain-colored seconds
from all the clocks that ever were.
Look again
and find yourself changed
and changing, now the bewildered honey.

Where do the gone things go?
Things don't die or remain damaged
but return.
Let us not let go
ever.

James and Michael James Trace the Past

In the open vistas of Rawnshinshare's old hills,
breath comes to the graves of those who've slept.

By green ponds lying deep and murmuring soft,
where speckled frogs open their throats in duets,
the mute church spoke of ancestors unknown or unsaid.
Then a rosebud unfurled its tender red petals.
A world opened loud-brilliant in the afternoon sun.
And lambs bleated their birth songs and leapt.

Finally known—written in cursive, in inks indelible,
deliberate and legible to any who look,
a worn leather book opens cold stormy tides
to pages stained with snow-ancient weeping,
to punishment and conquest of women now flown.

Here: Michael James Quinn born to Aisling Bernadette,
May 2, 1960, in the Bally House of Milk and Bread.
Unwed. Father unknown or father unsaid. And a death.

When stars falling from the blue-dark heavens
are swept away by the blush of dawn, the balm
of the opened morning can wrap the wet clay
and prickly nettles with its warmth. The kettle's on.
And the open hob's grown hot. Sweet rain hides
in the fleece of bedraggled lambs near One Man's Path.
Take care where you walk.

Black tea is asking the weary bee in the cowslips
to share its honey.
Tread softly because you tread on my dreams,
James says. But let me tell you about your mother.

Notes

These notes help explain some details of the poems. Included here are some simplified URL links for readers wishing to explore further.

1. "The Meaning of Sean Nós"
Sean nós singing (Irish for 'old style') is unaccompanied, traditional Irish vocal music usually performed in the Irish language. It usually involves very long melodic phrases differing greatly from traditional folk singing found elsewhere in Ireland. A beautiful example:
https://bit.ly/43Nm5sQ

2. "Ten Commandments to the Women of Holy Catholic Ireland, 1959"
These "commandments" as written are the author's extrapolation of popularly held concepts and social norms of the time as described in the research books written by actual members of Mother and Baby Homes and Irish Laundries. This is not an official dictate.

3. "Into the Mother and Baby Home"
Saint Agnes is widely known as the patron saint of young girls. She is also the patron saint of chastity, rape survivors, and the Children of Mary. She is often represented with a lamb, the symbol of her virgin innocence, and a palm branch, like other martyrs.

The epigraph is an erasure of the poem, "The Garden of Love" by William Blake in *Songs of Experience.*

Tea brack is a traditional Irish breakfast quickloaf made with warm mixed spices and sweet raisins that have been soaked in strong tea.

4. "James, Broken"
In Celtic mythology, the Rowan tree is called the Traveler's Tree because it's believed to prevent those on a journey from getting lost.

5. "From Ponytail to Chopped"
It was a usual practice to change the names of the women entering a
Mother and Baby Home as what happens in this poem.

Before the Fifth Amendment of the Constitution Act 1972 was approved
and signed into law on January 5, 1973, the state of Ireland recognized a
special position of the Holy Catholic Apostolic and Roman Church as the
guardian of the Faith professed by the great majority of the citizens.
'Special position' granted the church significant influence over law,
education, healthcare, cultural life, and basic social services, and included
the Garda Síochána, the national police and security service of Ireland.

6. "New Friends"
These questions are asked by the priest at the beginning of every Catholic
wedding ceremony. After being asked whether children will be accepted,
the words, "and bring them up according to the law of Christ and his
Church," has been purposefully left off this poem.

7. "Aisling Tells All: One Ordinary Girl on One Extraordinary Day"
The word feg is a commonly used slang word for a cigarette, and
"Sweet Afton" was the name of a brand of short cigarettes which were
manufactured by P.J. Carroll & Company, Ltd in Dundalk, Ireland. The
name comes from the poem "Sweet Afton" by Robert Burns. That poem
celebrates a river.

"C'mere t'me" is a colloquial Irish expression which means "listen to
me—I have something to tell you." The phrase always precedes the
intended information.

8. "The Earth Overturns"
"[B]etween 1925 and 1961, 796 children died at the St Mary's mother and
baby home, run by nuns from the Bon Secours order—but there were no
burial records. Many are believed to have ended up in the former sewage
facility. "It became a handy way to dispose of them," [Catherine] Corless
told the *Observer*. "They didn't have to account for the deaths. They

didn't want anyone to know. All this time those poor little remains were disintegrating."
bit.ly/3G42POw

The entire song of *Anach Cuain* can be heard in Irish at
bit.ly/3TrE5CX

9. "All the Voices Silenced"
The song, *Amhrán Mhuighinse*, The Song of Maínis (aka, Mweenish Island), can be heard in Irish at
bit.ly/3SSQIH7

The song is about a woman choosing her burial place.

On February 23, 1943, 35 girls and 1 adult died in a fire at St. Joseph's Orphanage and Industrial School (Main St., Cavan) which was established in 1869 by the Sisters of the Poor Clares. Details are at
bit.ly/4kK2r6S

10. "Aisling Speaks"
Just as Aisling was "erased" in many ways, this poem is an erasure of a poem by Katharine Tynan, 1859-1931, an Irish writer of novels and poetry who sometimes wrote under the name Katharine Tynan Hinkson after her marriage. Her work focused on the treatment of shop girls, unmarried mothers, infanticide, capital punishment, and the education of the poor.

11. *"Come with us, dear Michael"*
This poem rewrites the poem, "The Stolen Child," by William Butler Yeats.

A changeling is an infant believed to have been secretly substituted by the faeries for the parents' real child. Sometimes the changeling was a piece of wood or a bundle of sticks magically made to resemble the kidnapped child. A foundling is an infant abandoned by its parents and found and cared for by others.

£1000 in 1960 Ireland is worth about $33,000 today. At that time, donations from prospective parents were expected during adoption negotiations.

12. "In the Pubs, Nightly"
The line "whatever it is that a wound remembers" is from "Small Prayer" by Weldon Kees.

The endline is from the song, *Grace* written in 1985 by Frank O'Meara (melody) and Sean O'Meara (lyrics). It tells the story of the marriage of Grace Gifford and Joseph Plunkett in Kilmainham Gaol just hours before his execution in 1916 following the Easter Rising. The story and song can be heard at
bit.ly/4kK2r6S

13. "Called Home"
Hungry Grass (Fear Gortach) is believed to be a faery curse which makes those who stand near it extraordinarily hungry. Meadows and paths known to grow it are still avoided.

The italicized lines are excerpts from "The Stolen Child" by William Butler Yeats who had visited the lovely glens and waterfalls in County Leitrim.

14. "Imperfect Lambs"
The line, 'Useless to think you'll park and capture it' is from the poem, "Postscript," by Seamus Heaney.

15. "Eleanór a Rún"
The song *Eleanór a Rún* can be heard in Irish at
https://bit.ly/3ZAgzHE

16. "As If the Dirt Was Just Sugar"
In Irish myth, there is another otherworldly realm called Tech Duinn ("House of the Dark One"). It was believed that the souls of the dead travelled to Tech Duinn—perhaps to remain there forever or perhaps waiting for their final destination in the Otherworld.

The early peoples believed in reincarnation. Druids believed that sins committed in a previous life could be made up for in the next. It was the cycle of nature.

The word "tuatha," pronounced TOO-ah, is an Old Irish word that means people, tribe, or clan.

17. "Putting Pieces Together"
A cento borrows lines from other poets and arranges them to make a new, original poem. Poems / Poets in order of first appearance in this poem:

"Black Cherries" by W.S. Merwin
"Contemplations at the Virgin de la Caridad Cafeteria, Inc." by Richard Blanco
"Night Mirror" by Li-Young Lee
"Pied Beauty" by Gerard Manley Hopkins
"In Passing" by Matthew Shenoda
"The Visitation" by Traci Brimhall
"The Seconds" by Derek Sheffield
"In Childhood" by Kimiko Hahn

18. "James and Michael James Trace the Past"
"Rawnshinshare" is a fictional town name anglicized from the Irish arán sinséir meaning ginger- or ancestral bread.

The line, 'Tread softly because you tread on my dreams' is from "Aedh Wishes for the Cloths of Heaven" by William Butler Yeats.

One Man's Path is a very narrow hiking ridge on the top of the cliff side of Slieve Liag which can only be traversed by skilled walkers.

Sources for Research

- *Foster* by Claire Keegan
- *Girl in the Tunnel* by Maureen Sullivan
- *Small Things Like These* by Claire Keegan (book and movie)
- *The Baby Snatchers* by Mary Creighton
- *The Adoption Machine* by Paul Jude Redmond
- *The Light in the Window* by June Goulding
- *The Missing Children* documentary, which can be found at **https://bit.ly/3TsEQM3**

Details about tracing birth records of people in one of Ireland's Mother and Baby Homes can be found on these sites:

https://bit.ly/3ZAcMKh

https://bit.ly/3HMOnv1

Acknowledgments

My everlasting gratitude goes to my editor and dear friend, Ginny Lowe Connors, who first read this manuscript and encouraged it into being. And also, to Cynthia Blackburn from my Writers in Progress workshop who read the manuscript so carefully and proved its worth for American readers unfamiliar with contemporary Irish history.

As ever, my workshop groups, including Partners in Poetry and the Farmington Valley Chapter of the Connecticut Poetry Society, have seen many of these poems in their raw beginnings and helped me to polish them. I can't thank each of them enough.

The January 2025 cohort of the Sancho Panza Literary Society heard the first series of these poems at Trinity College in Dublin, Ireland, and my dear friend and fellow Irish student, Rose Malone, offered to read the seedling manuscript. I will be forever grateful for her kind attention to this work, for her suggestions, and for telling me her own memories of these days.

I am deeply indebted to the editors of the following journal that first published, sometimes with different wordings or titles, these poems:

Ink Nest Poetry   "As If Young Love Could Heal"
                "Love Letter Folded into Eighths"

About the Author

D. Walsh Gilbert is a dual citizen of the United States of America and the Republic of Ireland. Her poetry collections include *Ransom, imagine the small bones, Finches in Kilmainham* and *Misneach* (all, Grayson Books), *Once the Earth had Two Moons* (Cerasus Poetry), *[M]AR[Y]* (Kelsay Books), *Deirdre* (Impspired), *Bleat & Prattle* (Clare Songbirds Publishing House), and *no mother but the sky* (The Poetry Box). Her poems appear widely in poetry journals online and in print. She serves on the board of the Riverwood Poetry Series and as associate editor of the *Connecticut River Review*, published by the Connecticut Poetry Society.

Gilbert lives in Farmington, Connecticut on a former sheep farm at the foot of the Talcott Mountain near the watershed of the Farmington River. Previously, this area was the homeland of the Tunxis and Sukiaugk peoples; it's near the oldest site of human occupation in Connecticut, dating back 12,500 years. She welcomes turkey, bear, and bobcat as daily visitors from the forest behind her home, writes every day, and visits her family in County Monaghan, Ireland as often as possible.